Paper Camera

Paper Camera

Poems, Poets, and Poetry

Joyce Sutphen

Nodin Press

ISBN: 978-1-947237-67-4

Library of Congress Control Number: 2025936921

Cover art: Henri Fantin-Latour / *Woman reading*, 1861,
courtesy Musée d'Orsay, Paris, France.

Published by

Nodin Press
210 Edge Place
Minneapolis, MN 55418

This book is dedicated to my readers, fellow poets, artists, choreographers, and composers, and to all of you who have given my poems a place in your lives.

Contents

Three

Four

The Paper Camera

It turned out to be perfect for those
times when a Nikon would have

been too conspicuous or awkward
for the situation, which might require

crawling on hands and knees
through a narrow tunnel,

or putting on a face mask and flippers
and diving into a wreck. It could

focus on one thing and evoke something
else; it spoke the language of color,

shadow, and depth of field—it loved the light,
sun, moon and stars, lamp and candle.

The paper camera translated the world
into images and imagined new worlds.

It did this frame by frame, each click
the shudder of worlds opening wide.

It caught the body coming through the rye,
the cuckoo flying overhead. It brought

what was far away close and what was
close closer. It made of motion a moment.

One

Why There Is Poetry

Because there are colors, even in winter,
before the rusty buds appear on gray twigs

at the end of the branch, before the blue
drifts in through clouds split open like cut-silk

and the golden sun lights up the bleached
grass in the meadow. Because of creatures

crossing the lawn when we look out at dusk—
a procession of deer without antlers,

a single pheasant in his embroidered vest,
because someone needed to hear the sound

of someone laughing and someone else had
a joke to tell and because there are stars

so far away that we cannot see them,
which is another reason for poetry.

What Poetry Does for Us

Wonders. A world of good. Makes us feel young
again. Almost as good as being in

Florida or New Mexico, knowing
that it's 20 below back home. It cheers

us up, calms us down, brings us back around
to those faces we'd forgotten about;

reminds us of why we love the night sky,
tells us why we decided not to leave

the town along the river that will flood
one of these years—but not this time; this time

the dikes are holding, this time we'll all be
safe, and we'll breathe a huge sigh of relief—

which is another thing it does for us:
chases away the nightmares with a song.

Why We Are Afraid of It

Because it makes things up—
love, forgiveness, the town that holds
the river back,

and because people admire it for its
foolishness, and we have worked
so hard for our wisdom,

because it says one thing and means
another, because it never stops
talking about death.

For the same reason we are afraid
of taking the day off,
or ordering sushi,

because we can't imagine the poet
at a baseball game
or watching TV,

because we think we would have to be
someone else to read it, that it would
never be what we wanted,

and because we have never been certain
about what we wanted, and
poetry might tell us.

It's All Good

I like a poet who reminds me of things
I didn't know I knew, but I did,

and I am fond of those who make me want
to go home and write the poem only

I can write. Best of all is the poet
who can bring us all together—the way

Dylan did with songs like "Blowing in
the Wind" and "Masters of War."

I'm crazy about dead poets; they do
things with words to make lines so

beautiful that I wish that I had written them!
"Poets are the unacknowledged legislators

of the world." That's Percy Bysshe Shelley,
and I adore a poet who gives me hope.

Reading

All day, I was eating up the pages,
my eyes and ears filling with luscious

words like wild berries in a tin can,
some for the story—for usefulness—and

some just to put in my mouth for sweetness.
Long before the sun lit up the meadow,

I turned on the light and opened the book.
When the sun was on one side of the house,

I was deep into another heart, far
into another time and place—clean gone.

You would have seen a body moving from
one location to another: at the table, resting

head in hand as she read, or in the kitchen,
eyes on the page, or walking in the yard like

Lady Hamlet—out of the air and in-
to this other world, this miraculous

incarnation that begins with single letters
and ends in the voice of the one you love.

How to Memorize a Poem

[Long silence]

Honestly, I've forgotten how I did it.
Magic is required, that much I know.

A little repetition goes a long way;
point the car in the right direction

and begin with "Complacencies
of the peignoir." Go until you've reached the

"old chimera of the grave," and check
your map ... It's alright; you're still on track!

There's "April's green," and there those "wakened birds,"
who "test the reality of misty fields,"

followed by "Death, the mother of Beauty."

You finally get that, the reason
you spent all those hours getting it down,

word for word, was to
launch yourself out "on extended wing."

Finding the Names

Who first called it morning—
called that golden thing
climbing over the horizon, daylight?

Who was it first saw wings
and feathers and said bird?
Who dared call the tiger, tiger?

How many centuries went by
before someone divided time
into days and months?

Who named the minutes
and hours, over and over again—
who thought up eternity?

And what is the name for
knowing that even as the world
glows with light—as in

a Vermeer painting—it will
all disappear one day, the way
clouds dissolve into the blue.

Enough

That's enough. Thick line.
Straight toward you.
– Rolf Jacobsen

In the morning, the sun
floods the room
and lights up a row of books.

I pull one out,
looking for something
to carry into the day.

It doesn't take long,
and I have a line
about the moon, how it

"thumbs through the book
of night," looking
for someone to save.

I can do something with that.

My Native Tongue

These are the words I learned
in my mother's arms as she walked
me back and forth in the kitchen
and the light over the barn
was the only star we could see.

I learned "tractor" and "cow,"
and the sound each one made.
I learned that the dog said
"bow-wow" and the cat "meow."
"Go to sleep, she said—
and not "My little darling."

Recipe for a Poem

Take one cup of words and pour
them onto the page. Break open
a dozen old proverbs, and beat lightly.

Chop logic into fine pieces,
sauté in a sauce of
whimsy and imagination.

Bring all proclamations to
a boil, stir and let simmer
for at a century or two.

Pour into whatever sort of
stanza you have at hand
and bake at less than 451°

until something springs back
when you read it again. You are
surprised, and a little part of

the top of your head is missing.
Cool. Serve with ice-cream.

The Microwave Poem

By the time my pen hits the
paper, I already have less than five
minutes to write this poem—

well, only four minutes and
thirty-two seconds now,
and less than that when I look up

again, which is why I have
decided to keep my eyes
on the page and ignore the little

electric whirlwind of the oven
as it turns my spicy Thai chicken
slowly on the glass carousel,

and I am not watching how
the seconds, like sand, are
counting themselves backwards

although just now, when I looked
over, I saw that I have less than
ten seconds to the beep (beep, beep).

Etch A Sketch

White rain
under my footsteps,
cold mitten brushing clear
the windshield.

By evening,
the playground
and the garden disappear;
nothing left but moonscape.

Shadows of deer
grazing in the marsh
etch a trailing line

for the falling sky
to erase and
erase
each morning.

PowerPoint Poem

This is the first line.
You can look at it while
I read it out loud.

Whatever is in the poem
will stay in these lines,
and you will be able

to look back and see if
you heard it right, and
whatever I am going

to say will appear just
ahead of what I am
saying right now

so you can decide
whether you want
to keep reading

or not, in which case
you will not be reading
this line and therefore

will not know that
we are very close
to the end of the poem,

and that this is the first
line in the last stanza, and
that this is the last one.

Invention

I had an idea for a poem,
but I lost it to the phone

ringing its little head off
in the bottom of my purse.

Then another idea occurred
like trash in an empty lot

or like a leaf unfurled.
I'm not afraid of leaving here—

it's just that I keep missing
the boat, the train, the bus.

My heart goes out to that guy,
who fell asleep and dreamt

of Xanadu, but then he heard
a knocking at the door,

and that was all he wrote that
day and even long after.

How Do You Know If You're a Poet?

Yippee!
I'm a poet, and I know it.
Hope I don't blow it!
– Bob Dylan

One answer is that if you have to ask,
you probably aren't, or that you just

know when you know and that's it. Poets
rarely admit that they are poets, that

they spend endless hours working on those
little things William Carlos Williams

called "verbal contraptions"—machines
made of words and spaces, arranged with

a combination of sense and sound.
If you're a poet, you know when the right

words are in the right places, and you love
certain poems so much that you memorize

them. You know when to end a line and when
to keep going. Brevity is the soul

of wit, and you aren't afraid to kill
your darlings, and if your poem isn't

going anywhere, you know how to wait;
you know how to start all over again.

How to Write the Perfect Love Poem

Turn your cell phone off; tell
yourself you have all day.
Take the day off.

Don't make comparisons,
don't use hyperbole,
don't get cheesy.

Try not to imagine his
eyes and voice. Forget
everything he said.

Don't try to be Shakespearean—
you know—with that little
trick that makes the line you're

writing right now become the line
that is going to last forever
(just because you said it would).

Thank You for Coming

I mean that. You could be so many other
places right now: Your own quiet study,
your neighbor's new hot tub, Arizona.

Thank you for listening—or at least you
look as if you are. That helps.
I have a poem about listening I could read.

Maybe later. Thank you for imagining
what I could have said earlier—something
much better than what I am saying now.

Thank you for letting me start over
again. There. We'll begin at the beginning
and go back all the way to the ending

and thanks for being here. How long has it been?
Years. I was so much younger then; you were
younger too. Thanks for not mentioning it.

Thanks for buying my book; you wouldn't
have had to, unless you're a collector. Ah!
Well, in that case, I'll sign and date it:

"Thank you for coming; it's always a pleasure!"

Born to Be Wild

First, turn off the radio, and sit
quietly at your desk until you hear

something moaning inside of you. It's a
poem that's lost its way; it's a sonnet

in distress, a villanelle full of villains,
a ghazal leaping among the gazelles.

Check your location and approach with caution.
Wear gloves. Do not feed the poem, no matter how

it begs, do not let it off the leash.
Don't pick it up or call it your "little

darling." This poem is a wild animal
and should be treated like one!

Two

Mr. Muse

When he comes, he comes without warning;
when he goes, he never says goodbye.
Ask not, receive not, he won't say why.

He arrives by train, he drops out
of the blue. He's got wax on his
shoulder blade, hawk in his eye.

When he sings, he sings low-down deep,
like a wheel, he turns round in the words.
There's nothing he wouldn't say.

He's a wine-dark road, he blows in
from the cold. He's a glance in this
direction. Watch out! Here he comes!

Learning How

It took many days of trying,
many days of failing (failing better!),

but at last I learned how to climb
out of the water onto the smooth back

of the lake where I could skim
—back and forth—across the

middle of the wake that spread (like a fan!)
behind my uncle's speedboat.

I wanted to write my name on the middle
of that lake as proof that I had walked on

water; I wanted to lean so far out
that I would shimmer

with phosphorescence before I
broke into something like rain.

The Basic Plot

I keep forgetting that history
isn't like the stories I love,

that the man on the scaffold
won't be reprieved just as

the executioner slips the
black sack over his head—

that Guinevere, tied to the
stake, won't be rescued by

Lancelot on a white horse,
as the crowd presses in

with all its fiery torches.
And I forget that in real life

things happen that are so
shocking and wrong that—

were I watching them on
TV—would make me switch

the channel to something more
pleasant. I keep forgetting

that I am not a miracle, that
I have no superpower, and that

all of this has happened before,
and no one has ever survived.

On Wednesday

When we woke, we heard
the sound of rain—constant rain—

a whisper along the edges of
the roof, a steady threading

through in the air.
We leaned on pillows

and remembered
the night before the night before.

We planned (even though we knew
such things must come as naturally

as leaves to a tree). Then you got
the pangram in one, and the wordle

in two. You beat the bot, but
when the skies cleared, it was just

another day, filled with worries,
little gray donkeys packed and

ready, carrying enough supplies
to last us into winter and beyond.

Not Remembering

I remember the word for chair.
I want to say—I'm just not interested anymore.

– Louise Glück

I wouldn't even call it forgetting—
it's simply not remembering, not even

making an effort to imprint the names
of anyone I meet these days as I shake

their hands and look deeply into their very
blue eyes, which remind me of that actor—

the one who played the guy who ate the eggs,
which reminds me of a poem about

a girl reading a book stained with something
that looks like egg-salad, a book that I

once read chapter by chapter in a store
because my mother wouldn't let me buy

a book banned by the church we belonged to
(something big, filled with incense and statues).

Too Much Information

Don't tell me everything.
I don't want to know
how it all turns out in the end,

and I especially don't want to know
how you felt the moment
it happened

and how what happened was so
unexpected that it made you
feel like—well, whatever it was

don't tell me, I don't want to know,
because I want to be able to
imagine being you, having something

like that happen to me,
and I want to be able to wonder
what I would do then and

how it feels being inside
you when even you aren't quite
sure what is coming next,

and please, whatever you do,
don't tell me the ending.
I don't ever want to know.

That Poem

I am not writing that poem now because
I am writing this other one—the one

that is standing behind me, very still,
hardly breathing. As long as you are here,

as long as you keep listening, I'll keep
writing this poem, the one that wants to be

a spaceship (something out of *Flash Gordon*!)
or the words of the last human being.

I am not writing that poem because now
is not the end of the world. No—now

is just a way of saying this moment
is all you have. Listen. That poem is

about the future: rockets and robots
and beyond to infinity. This poem is

trying to decide where to go next and
how to say what has become obvious.

Not for Publication

This poem doesn't want to happen,
this poem is avoiding the page, this poem

knows that it makes nothing happen, which is
another way of saying nothing left

to lose. This poem stays up nights watching
Russian Dolls in order to understand

that she and the woman with the red hair
are one, and that whatever happens there

happens here, but this poem doesn't
want to talk about that, doesn't want you

at the door, with your bouquet of wilted
flowers. This poem would like to make itself

into a silence, to leave the party
now, just as the police are arriving.

Down in the Word

When we turned the corner, we were coming
into words, sprouting syllables the way

branches turn to leaf, and one of us was
humming an old song, something cool, jazzy—

the kind of song that helped us through the last
few years. This is how we began: pulling

chairs up to the table, letting the day
fall away, hearing night come slowly on,

watching words (worlds!) slide down the margins, space
between the stanzas, our breath drawn in lines

of ink, our fingers tapping paragraphs
to the sound of long riffs, tempo set by

the drum that is this room, that is this page
where you listen, playing it over now.

Just Listen

Imagine that one morning you get up
without turning on the radio or

checking your email. You simply listen to
the sound of the world: wheels on the highway,

an engine revving up or shifting down,
three motorcycles, and then a lull—

the sound of someone walking in the leaves,
and a bird (you don't know its name, but you

know you've been hearing it without really
hearing it for years), and now you notice

wind in the branches and a leaf doing
somersaults across the flat roof near

your window, and just then—did you hear it?
—a door opening somewhere in the house.

I Said

Clock,
what do you count when you are not
keeping time? Clock, what is the reason, what
is the rhyme?'

Stone, I said,
How did you smooth and flatten like that?
How did you gray the same way
each one of you, too many to count?

Leaf,
I said. Grief is your middle name; sorrow
is not the same thing, and sadness is
nothing at all.

Love, I said,
you were there all the while, you with
that wonderous smile and your sandal
unbuckled.

Errata

The author of this paper, he wrote,
is a hopeful romantic (and he should
have added, does not know the
difference between conquer and concur).

He takes certain things for granite;
he fears the distinction of death
and the ineffable onset of age.
Morality casts a long dark shadow.

For him, one word is inextinguishable
from the next; they are simultaneous
and buried as leaves upon the shore.
He sees a whirlwind in each brain.

There is a curtain of truth in all he says,
a micro-chasm in each distance he gives.
Someday he will unravel the earth, tread
by tread, to detect its wolves and warbles.

Inter-Text-Mix

This text is talking to
that one: in the long hot
afternoon, it is

leaning over a table
of contents,
checking indexes and

leafing through the
chapters one by
one. Pieces of this text

slip into that one:
a word here,
a name there.

They've heard of texts
that swallow
other texts whole

and texts that
disappear into the margins
of another one.

That fat novel over there
used to be
a short lyric,

and that short story
was once a
"Do Not Enter" sign.

How voluminous they've
become, now that word
is talking to word,

now that sentences are
never over, and nothing can
ever end, period.

Reading the Papers

After a while I learned to read
those wounded sentences, to see
the letters hidden in the words.

Everything that was upside down,
I turned right again, translating freely.
Everything out of place,

I rearranged. All I needed to hear
was the smallest stay against
confusion. I stopped trying to

make changes, but took it as
it came, then let it go
again, straining to hear

(above the clunking gears)
the clear bell of thought.

This Poem

This poem is getting old—
old enough to go out into the world
and do something other than looking
poetic, hanging around in a book.

And this poem is old enough to drink,
but it doesn't; this poem was there when the
famous poet got drunk and gave a terrible
reading. This poem never wants to do that.

This poem is about to join some others
in an anthology of nature poems. It will be
somewhere towards the end, next to a poem
by Robert Frost and back-to-back with

Emily Dickinson, whose poem arrived
a ribbon at a time in a rainbow
of color. This poem can't believe its
luck; this poem feels like an imposter.

Most poems are slightly neurotic, and some
are superstitious; others are quite ambitious
for honors and awards, but going where it
has to go is all this poem is about.

This poem has never been a song, and now
it will be filled with voices—soprano

alto, tenor, baritone, bass. This poem
will be divided into measures, and parts

of it will be repeated while others
will make a melody for a gospel choir
to shout and sing in harmony, holding
each word for a long soulful Lord, Lord.

Crossword

As in: he was cross that night and said things
he didn't mean—words that threw the puzzle

off, but she kept at it; every time
she came into the kitchen, she'd stop and

read a clue out loud: "What's seven letters,
begins with a D and is someplace you

could be imprisoned forever?" "And what
about thirteen down: reminders of past

fights? Hint: five letters, and the first is S."
"What's Spanish for a person disappeared?"

We learned another word for destiny
is fate, and that certainty often comes

too late in a sort of "coup de_____."
The choices seemed so_______.

One More Thing

I need a break I think—it's getting late,
but before we go to bed my darling dear,
I have to finish one more thing . . . please wait

up for me—don't turn out the light; I hate
to tiptoe in when you're asleep—it's clear
I need a break. I think it's getting late—

it's hard to tell; my life's in such a state
I sometimes wonder who's in charge here!
(I have to finish one more thing please.) Wait—

did I ever tell you about the fate
of my last project, "The Comic King Lear"?
I need a break (I think). It's getting late.

You have that look I've come to know—"irate"
might be putting it too mildly—I fear
I best not finish one more thing! Please wait

a second more. I will not hesitate—
I'll come to bed directly with such cheer
you'll need a break. I think it's getting late.
I have to finish one more thing—please wait!

Three

Counting My Losses

First I lost a little sleep, lost some
papers, lost the sunglasses
you gave me that were like the ones
I lost in London. That was my deal—
losing mittens, losing keys.

Then I lost interest in theories
and conundrums; I would begin
the latest article on Lacan and find
myself drifting, without whatever
it was that used to make me care.

Along the way I lost my dreams,
my hat, and the sails to the little
boat I kept in the harbor.
I lost my handwriting—which some
said was beautiful but few could read—

and then I began to lose my balance.
I lost my voice and my smile,
lost my place in the line,
in the book I was reading, lost my fear
at the airplane's open door.

What I Kept

I kept my smile and the desire
to make the person walking towards me
looking worried or weary, smile,

and though my jaws tightened,
and my tongue stumbled on the
words, I kept my way of talking.

For reasons I can't explain,
I kept my memory of certain poems,
but lost all sorts of detail: the names and

addresses of my six brothers, the poet
who wrote *Paradise Lost* and a sonnet
that ends with "They also serve who only

stand and wait." Milton. That's his name, and now
I won't forget it until I forget
that I forgot it once before.

At the end, when there wasn't anything
I could do but watch the dissolution
of my mind and body, I kept hope,

the thing with feathers (you know the lines!)
singing and singing to keep us warm.

At the Colony

You'd have a hundred poems already,
unless you can only write in noisy
coffee shops, surrounded by investment bankers.

As for the poet who lives here—
the pileated woodpecker—he is indeed
very large, with a bright red crest.

In the morning, he is out early, his
chisel-like beak drilling through bark
and wood. He eats insects.

I do not know what other birds
live in these pines. The woodpecker
is ubiquitous.

Now the snow is falling and it is
very quiet out there, quiet
enough to write a poem.

Another Day in Paradise

There is so much embellishment involved.
What you've heard is not even partly true.

We must suffer for our singing,
and the doorstep is always empty.

The town is not a place that you would go,
there is no hardware store,

but you could stay at your desk all day.
There are no bells ringing you in for dinner,

no whisky on the shelf. No one sleeps
with anyone here—it's a modern

monastery, without prayers,
without solace.

You might like it here (there are some that do);
expect nothing, and let it be enough.

Your Poems

I like the way the subject line is
always the same: "Poem," it says,

followed by "No body," so either the
poem is a spirit and has no body,

or there is nothing there but poem
(Our Daily Poem) which we read

without replying. Forgive us—your
poems are like those plums that

Dr. Williams mentioned—so sweet
that we can't help but eat them—or

they are bread, fresh from the oven
of the day—your day—whatever it

turned out to be when you paused
to write down that word "Poem."

After Another Poem

You know there is always another one—
Like a breath—or a wave coming in.
–Tim Nolan

Yes, I do know there will always be
another poem, that even as I write

these lines about the poem you sent
this afternoon when the sun (gone now)

was shedding its warmth over the path,
even then you were onto another poem,

this time an ode to your blue socks—
another one I did not fail to read

(which is just to say that even though
you think I don't open them, I do).

In the poem about the blue socks,
I liked the assertion of happiness,

especially after yesterday's poems,
which I have to say, were downers.

Thing is, I've started counting on your poems;
they're my daily feed, my ticket to the

moment, words on a wire. They're what
is found there—what I haven't yet thought,

what I turn to without knowing—
the substance of things unknown.

So write something hopeful, something
so amazing it knocks your socks off—

those blue ones you wrote about,
the ones the color of Paul Newman's eyes,

write one of those poems about summers
in Minneapolis when you were a kid, and

how you love clouds (even now) passing
high above us—way off to the south.

Sitting in Whitman's Chair

He has that ease now, that expansive
all-encompassing ease that you will assume

what he does, that you will pause when he
pauses—listening to his thoughts, which

are also your thoughts, and after all the years
his subjects are multitudinous; he contains all

that he was, is and will be, but for now (this
present moment), he wants you with him

as he looks out the window at the traffic
on Franklin Avenue or at the bird that

just landed on the ledge of the window—
bird, window, traffic, sky—it no longer

matters. He is at ease, he loafs, and invites
his soul to celebrate, to sound his barbaric

yawp over the parking lot where an old
man struggles with a grocery cart filled

with morning papers and a hawk
swings over, looking for home.

About the Stars

The poem, this morning, was one
we both heard Louis read last summer

at Tom and Freya's house near Stillwater …
or did we hear it last fall at Connie and Phil's

place in Mendota Heights when Patricia
arrived with those beautiful red journals?

I recall that Michael and Lisa were there
and also Tim and Kate, and (of course)

Tom and Freya, as guests this time …
or was that the day it was so hot that

Louis and Tim brought their lawn chairs
right down to the edge of the lake and

sat there talking for a long time with the waters
shimmering beyond them like a celestial city …

Now I think that none of these were the day
we first heard Louis's poem about the stars. No,

I believe it was long before that, in a house
none of us owned, deep in the woods north of Duluth,

and I'm sure that Ann, who I haven't mentioned,
but was always there, brought out one of her pies,

and Louis pulled a folded piece of paper from a pocket
and began to read (very slowly, in that voice we

loved so much) the poem we heard this morning—
the one that made us laugh until we cried.

Having a Beer with Louis Jenkins

Billy Collins was there too, and what
we talked about and what kind of beer it was—

it's all gone now, except that I remember
you were memorizing the sonnet that begins:

"Some glory in their birth, some in their skill,"
and Louis casually said "The Snowman"

by Wallace Stevens in a way that convinced
me forever that he'd arrived at his ideas

about the line after careful consideration
and knowledge, and from that day on, I have

regarded the Louis Jenkins prose poem
as equal to the sonnet and villanelle;

in fact, in the hands of the master,
something like this happens: you see a man

standing on the deck of the QE2
handcuffed, shackled and stuffed into a trunk

which is crisscrossed with chains and tossed
into the Atlantic. You wait (for hours,

it seems), and then—just as the crowd begins
to turn away— he breaks through the waves, laughing.

Looking Good

After the words had settled into place,
my poem was looking good. Her lines

were even, and in that lighting a slight
rhyme was almost discernible. She had

her tone under control, and all of her
metaphors were extended and worked

quite nicely with an idea that had
emerged in the second stanza and was

developing nicely in the fourth. Then,
without warning, everything collapsed.

Turned out my idea was an old one;
someone had already said the same thing

better. Turned out my poem had no there
there, but she was definitely looking good.

Riding the Highway with Emily

She wanted to drive—
and she drove very fast,
tired of the clip-clop
of Death's carriage.

Immortality sat in back—
seated-belted and
silently screaming at
every curve.

I barely noticed the school,
but Emily saw it—and
searched for Pink Floyd
on the MP3 player,

finding, instead, The Animals
and "The House of the Rising
Sun"—which we also passed,
along with a loaded gun

and a thing with feathers.
After that, we drove for hours,
until we saw the house
with its rooftop in the ground—

I had a feeling in my bones
(like zero), but she just nodded

and drove on. Since then, we've
only stopped for a certain slant of light.

On His Birthday

I would give Gerard Manley Hopkins
a kestrel hawk, a rose-mole stippled trout,

and a new row of poplars for the village.
I would play him a tape made on a hilltop

in the middle of America—his words, floating
over strange and wild keyboards, voices

looping into dappled harmony, pied piper.
On his birthday, I would take G. M. Hopkins

to the movies and afterwards out to dinner
at a Thai restaurant. I would say "Relax

Gerry, you worked much too hard in 1889;
forget about that stack of papers—darksome

chaff of sheer nothingness. Check out
Harry Potter, have a humungous bag of

hot buttered popcorn, and after that we'll
have pot-stickers and noodles.

I would want to give Hopkins a party
on his birthday. Yeats would be there

and Whitman too. Maybe Wallace Stevens
and Emily Dickinson—If I could convince

her to come. Elizabeth Bishop too.
I'd order cases of wine and have

Guinness on tap. My friends Connie
and Tim would both read him something

they'd written just for the occasion
On his birthday, I would ask him if it all

ended with a deep sleep and if there
was comfort there, under the whirlwind.

Which world do you remember best? I'd ask,
the one charged with the grandeur of God

or the mind's mountains, cliffs of fall?
When I brought out the cake, the candles
would give his face (ah bright!) a golden glow.

Eliot in the 60s

I grow old … I grow old
– J. Alfred Prufrock

This was the poem
most often on display
in the classrooms and
lecture halls of colleges
across the country

(like a patient etherized
on a table) when I fell in love
with poetry and the world
of sound and fury
in lines that became
my constant guide,

my obsession,
my possession of
a world without end,
endlessly whirling.

Why did we linger
in those rooms?
Where did the women go,
talking of Michelangelo?

And who was Prufrock
that he could hear
the mermaids singing?

Monkey Bird

The poem I was hoping to write
is still sleeping. What can I say?

It was up late, imagining ways
to please you. It turned into

a puppy and did tricks; it barked
and chased its tail on command.

"What a good little doggie," you said.
"Good dog, good puppy, good boy!"

The poem was so happy it wagged
its tail. All it wanted was attention,

but I was hoping for more—
I wanted something that had wings

and could attract a crowd.

When I Didn't Write a Poem

That was when I was always in the kitchen,
baking a batch of chocolate chip cookies,

or making whole wheat bread, and I seldom
wrote a poem when I was making dinner.

It's hard to write a poem when you are
vacuuming, folding wash, or ironing;

shopping for groceries is also not
conducive to immediate composition—

although what thoughts I had of Allen Ginsberg
as I pushed my poemless cart up and down

the aisles of the supermarket. Thinking about
Ginsberg reminds me that I never wrote

a poem about meeting Ferlinghetti in
the Chinese restaurant on 4th Street

or interviewing Margaret Drabble
for *The Minnesota Daily.* And what

will I write, now that I am sitting in
the dark, waiting for those poems to come home.

The Art of Revision

In the morning, I take out most
of what I put in last night.

I cross out everything that seems
excessive, every frill and fandango,

anything "fluffy"—a word that should
never again appear in a poem,

along with "blossom" and "awesome."
Once I have deleted everything

except the title—which now seems
to have been written by a poet

who knows something I don't,
I delete that as well and turn

the page. All that empty space
is waiting. What will I say?

Déjà Vu

"We have all been here before" is what we
say when we get the feeling that what

we are seeing is something that we saw
another time. Everything about it

is so familiar that we have to
shake the feeling that we are saying

words we said before, in the same doorway—
exactly like ones we said another time—

to the same person for the same reason,
and we don't know when, just that

it's happening again, exactly the way it
happened before in another place that keeps

winking at me when I see that the cat
sleeping on the couch isn't really there.

I Left This Page Blank

For you, whoever you are,
coming to it years or months
later, sometime not now, not
even knowing the whole story
but familiar with the characters
and some events of the time.

This is the page skipped over,
the one that follows all the
ragged attempts to set it down,
to set it right by saying nothing,
knowing that even that is
something too much.

This is the page of unspeakable
thoughts, things that have
haunted your dreams since you
were a child, things you
you will not hear or see
when you open the book—

This is the page left blank.

Four

Unerring Muse

Oh come live with me
and hang my words in air;

let each line be measured
by the joy it carries.

Let every sound and syllable
be what is needed.

I stumble and falter
but you, unerring one,

know (like the birds
singing away the darkness)

that nothing is changed
and everything has.

AUBADE

This is not about pen and ink, is it?
This is about where the ink isn't, like

holes in the ozone. This is about texts
that are written in water and in blood.

Nightly I hear the news, in voices from
across the world, telling me what happens

when I fall asleep, how quickly the earth
can shift, mountainsides sliding into valleys.

Don't pretend that you know the high altars,
the myths and stories that once cast shadows

by the fire. Don't imagine that you have
a voice where there has only been silence,

that the oat field can sing of things other
than the wild geese overhead, that the woods

hide more than the secrets of the fox and deer.
You know only snatches of the song born

of the prairie's forgetfulness, the mute
tongue of snow and ice, the earth turned over.

This is not about pages in a book,
books on a shelf. This is about the promise

of each morning and the pale fire licking
the darkness out of the bowl. Sun rising.

At This Age

– for Kenny

Always beginning with a question,
always wondering how long
anything will last.

Never wanting things to change,
never wanting anyone to grow old,
never anyone to die.

One day I hear about the death of a famous writer;
one day a baseball star flickers and goes out.
Then my friend of many years—

my friend, who first noticed
that once we were so young together,
my friend, who, when he told our stories

made them into legends, who loved
each person with an individual zeal
and lived so intensely

that we could feel him entering the room—
my friend died, and after that …
I forget … What was the question again?

Since You'll Never Read This

I like what's happened to you in my poems.
You stay where I put you; you don't question

the facts, and I never have to think about
you when I go grocery shopping. No Little

Debbie Cakes in this poem! If the lawn needs
mowing, you don't mow it, but since this is

a poem, the grass is always green, the leaves
are raked, and the rain gutters are filled with

words that will come in handy the next time
I write a villanelle. You have never

read my poems—that used to bother me,
but not anymore! I realize that means

I'm just talking, not trying to convince
anyone that what I'm saying is true.

The Short Bio

For days I couldn't get past the short bio—
the little paragraph that could sum up

my life, just-like-that: born, married, children.
Divorced, retired, and soon (no doubt) deceased.

There seemed little else worth writing about.
All of the things I had been trying

to remember were abandoned in favor
of the broad stroke—the pictogram of my life.

Behold a tree and the sun caught in it.
See the pipe and the sign under it which read

"This is not a pipe," in French. I wanted
to take snapshots of myself so that

I would remember the moments when I least
expected to see myself again; I wanted

to slip back into the body that never
suspected how much it was like a cloud.

Light the Light

Light the light that's long gone out,
burn the trees that held the sky,

plow the fields and let no harrow
ride the sillioned furrow down.

Send for counsel, and let your sorrow
speak the speeches still unwritten.

Smash all roads that rest on promises,
broken treaties and banished tongues.

Sing a song of silence, delivering
such truths as only stones can say;

watch the waking as it takes on
morning's bright and opulent wings.

At Phebe Hanson's Funeral

She would have loved it all: people
arriving in their Subarus, Hondas,
and Jeeps—so many cars that the huge
parking lot south of the church was
filled an hour before the service.

And it would have made her smile
(that generous all-out smile of hers)
to see the procession of people, dressed
in their best winter coats and sturdy
boots, make their way to the doors—

the oldest inching along, carefully
avoiding icy spots, concentrating,
while the children (not many, mostly
grandchildren) run down the carpeted
hallways, laughing. All because of her.

Oh, and she definitely would have loved
the service—"a real Norwegian
fandango" she would have whispered
in your ear if she had been there
singing the hymns she'd chosen,

listening to scriptures she wanted
us to hear—the ones about speaking
the truth and loving one another, but

the part that would have pleased her
the most was when Marly and Trish

read the poems, and the way that Death—
because he'd kindly stopped for her—
was as welcome there as any mother
would be, delivering her child
back into the air again.

Ascension Day

Today all things rise—the child
in her crib, the shoot of green grass
in the crack of the sidewalk, bread
in the pan.

They rise; they unfurl
and stretch. They lift and make themselves
tall; they grow weightless, they fill with
light
and shine above us,
ascending into the heavens,
bursting with power and happiness,
because the world,

which just a short while
before, had been inundated with grief,
mired in and weighed down with
mortal thoughts, is now

waking, as from a dream, looking
to the mountains, to the high towers
and to that perch within the soul
where hope is always singing.

One Way to Pray

This is what you must do:
get up early and go
(very quietly) to your desk.

Take out a notebook
and a good pen.
Write the morning out

in bird song and the
fragments of a dream
that has almost disappeared.

Think of the people you
love and imagine
their faces one by one

as the sun rises. This is just
another way of praying—
this is how you do it now.

The Productions of Time

Eternity is in love with the productions of time
– Blake

That's everything we know,
everything we are.
Flowers wilting in the vase,
skin wrinkling on the bone.

That's a cake in the oven,
players on a stage,
waiting for Godot,
that's the end of the year.

It's the clock stealing minutes,
The eight changing into nine,
The last shaft of sunlight
falling across the lawn.

It's what we were born for,
the ticking in the wrist,
the heart winding down,
the last word we spoke.

To Poetry

Today, I once again gave myself
to poetry and vowed I would work

without pay (though I knew what
I hoped to gain) so that I might

pay attention to each fleeting detail,
each leaf and shadow in the green

afternoon of a world filled
with change and death. Today

I said I would do what poetry
asked of me, which was simply

to look out the window and watch
the birds flit from branch to branch,

and perhaps, if I was lucky, see one
bite an angleworm in half. Today

I promised that I would walk on air
in honor of Seamus Heaney, who

also said (just before he died) that
we shouldn't be afraid, and I

remembered that when Borges went blind,
it happened very gradually, “like a

slow summer twilight,” he said,
and although his body

was never found, we think of Lorca
alive, and all the world green.

The Poem of Your Life

– for Ellie

Is waiting for you to come along—
some spring (or maybe it's winter)
in New York or Paris
on your way to meet someone
who will change everything
if you take the right train,
if you look up from the book you
are reading, if you say hello.

The poem never leaves you,
though sometimes it disappears
for months or turns into a cloud
or the moon. You forget about the
poem for many days, and then
one night the moon is shining over
snowy fields, and you follow it
(or it follows you), and that's

when you remember that the moon
once was a cloud that was once
a poem. The poem of your life
is the one with the camping gear;
she sleeps in a hammock whenever
she can and speaks very softly.
You'll have to listen carefully to
your poem, but it's always worth it—

she says what no one else says.
Everyone will want to read
the poem of your life; they'll
read it over and over until they
learn it by heart, which is the only
way to know a true poem,
and yours will be not only
true but beautiful and good.

It's a Mystery

–for Scott King

Then who will distribute
his elegant type

onto the blank pages
of the future? Who will

choose the perfect dragonfly
and set and proof the work

before it is locked in the chase
and placed in the press?

Who will ink the platen
with the midnight sky?

When the time comes
to gather the pages,

what words will light
the lamp in the spine?

A Poem for People Who Have Left Their Houses and Traveled Through the Dark to Hear Poetry

What is it you wanted to hear?
Something about the woods

lovely, dark, and deep?
Something about the sea (calm tonight)?

Songs of yourself—
whoever you are, old or

young again, waking at dawn
in the blue-black cold,

hearing your mother in the kitchen,
your father stoking the furnace,

and recognizing (at last)
their fierce devotion.

Was it love songs you wanted to hear?
Songs so sweet they make all creation shiver?

Or songs that sail you beyond
the sunset, beyond the western stars?

Is it Innisfree you want? A small cabin,
nine bean rows, and a hive for the honey-bee?

Or did you want a simple poem
where friends gather at dusk,

and each one brings something delicious
to a table filled with candlelight and wine?

Whatever it is you want, this poem
can only point to it, can only say

(like some unmasked, hapless wizard)
that you have had it with you all along,

that all you needed to do was listen very carefully—
the way you are doing right now.

Acknowledgments

First thanks go to Norton Stillman for including me in the great series of Nodin poets; it is wonderful to work together at last. Many thanks as well to John Toren, the man who gets everything together, the man who so deftly transforms the manuscript into a thing called a book. Thanks to Walt Cannon who typed emails and poems when my fingers wouldn't work, who motivates me to get out and walk every day, and who listened to these poems and many variations of these poems. Thanks Walt! I couldn't have done it without you. And, as always, I am grateful to Connie Wanek and Phil Dentinger, who in addition to reading proofs have proven to be the best of friends. Several of these poems first appeared on *The Writer's Almanac*, and I would like to thank Garrison Keillor for all he has done to bring individual poems to the people, and people to poetry. Since this is a book which is sometimes about writing poems, I also want to thank my writing teachers at the University of Minnesota, Patricia Hampl, Carol Bly, and Michael Dennis Browne. Thanks to my three back cover commenters, Deborah Keenan, Richard Terrill, and Margaret Hasse, all people whose work and poetic insights I deeply respect. I am grateful that they were willing to spend time with this book and notice things that I hope other readers appreciate too.

photo: Walt Cannon

Joyce Sutphen was raised on a farm in Stearns County, Minnesota. She is a professor emeritus of English at Gustavus Adolphus College and served as Minnesota's poet laureate from 2011 to 2021. She is the author of numerous books of poetry, among them *That Other Life*, *This Long Winter*, and *Carrying Water to the Field: New and Selected Poems.*